VITAMINS
ABC
AND OTHER
FOOD FACTS

Written by Eileen Palmer
Design and illustrations by Peter Read

Published by Amberwood Publishing Limited

Printed in the UK by Leicester Printers Limited

First published April 1992

Foreword

In this day and age there seems little danger of children who have a poor diet. But this is not the case. Whether due to convenience meals or a genuine lack of knowledge about food values, a significant proportion of children are getting sub-optimal nutrition.

There is growing concern among child nutritionists because essential vitamins and minerals are lacking from the modern diet.

It has recently become apparent that many young children are deficient in iron for example, which may be responsible for delayed growth and development. Some dietary fat is essential for children and adults alike, but too high a proportion in childhood may contribute to a higher rate of heart disease and cardiovascular problems seen in Western cultures. The prevention of illness has always been recognised as more effective and more efficient than a cure, improving the nutritional balance of the young would certainly seem to be an area where this is possible and could have a significant impact on common diseases that burden our society. In the A.B.C. of vitamins, Eileen Palmer introduces the basic essential vitamins needed for a balanced diet, and draws our attention to the mechanism of how food might work in a way that children will find interesting and amusing.

The illustrator, Peter Read, has beautifully drawn a selection of characters that will capture the imagination of small children and their parents. Vivid cartoon personalities nicely depict and parody naturally occuring compounds giving the reader some insight into the scientific basis of nutrition.

If these messages can be taught at an early age when eating habits are developing, children will be able to grow knowing their health and wellbeing is largely dependent on the foods they eat.

Dr George A. J. Crisp, MB BS

Introduction

Most children enjoy eating
without understanding the importance
of what they eat.

Food doesn't just stop us feeling hungry, it also
helps us grow and maintain a healthy body.

This alphabet of food facts will help
teachers, parents and children work
together to find out how essential
nutrients assist in proper growth
and development.

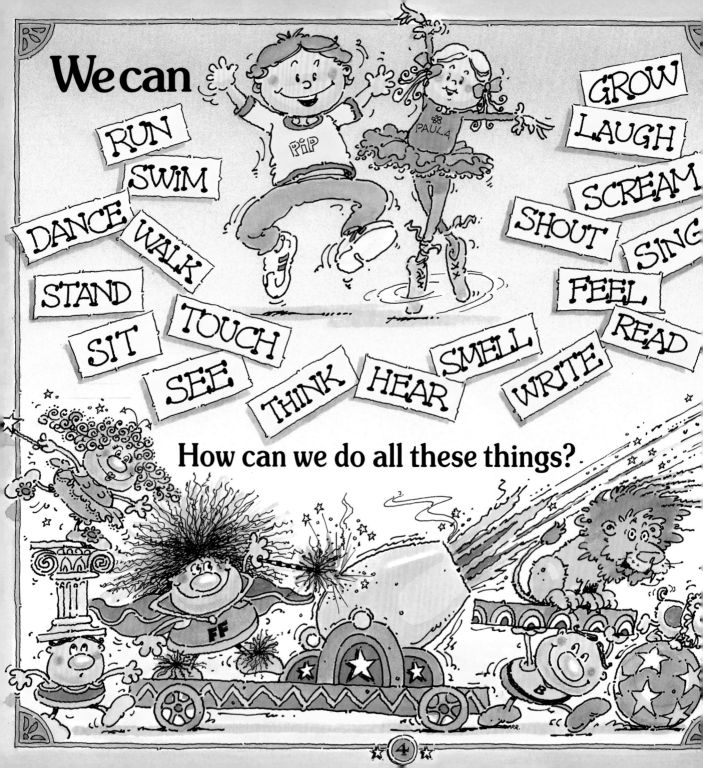

We can

RUN
SWIM
DANCE
WALK
STAND
SIT
TOUCH
SEE
THINK
HEAR
SMELL
WRITE
READ
FEEL
SING
SHOUT
SCREAM
LAUGH
GROW

How can we do all these things?

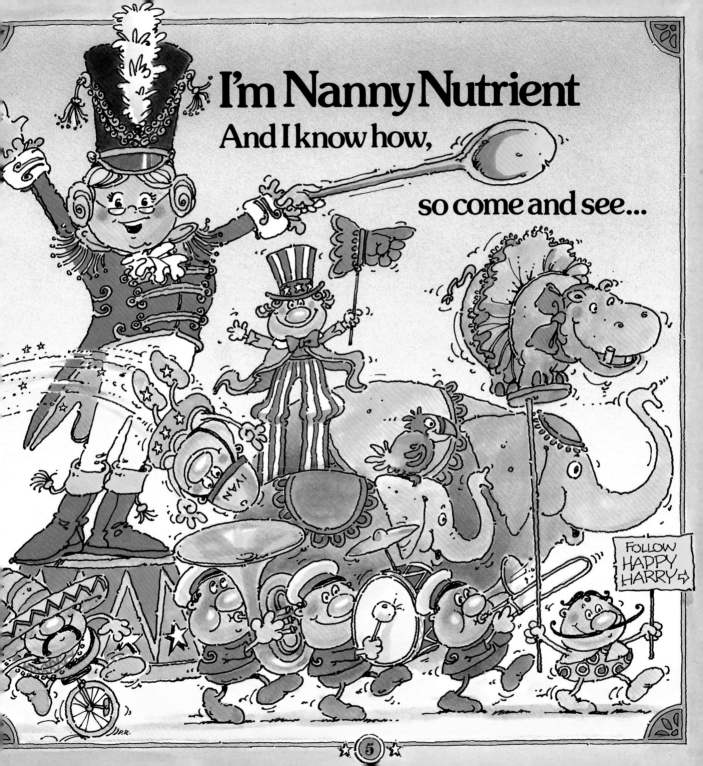

Annabelle Fairy

I am Vitamin A.

My real job is to look after your eyes and skin, but I also help you to see colours.

Another useful thing I do is to help prevent you getting coughs and colds.

Where is Vitamin A?

You will have Vitamin A if you eat fish, cheese, vegetables (especially green ones), salads, eggs, butter.

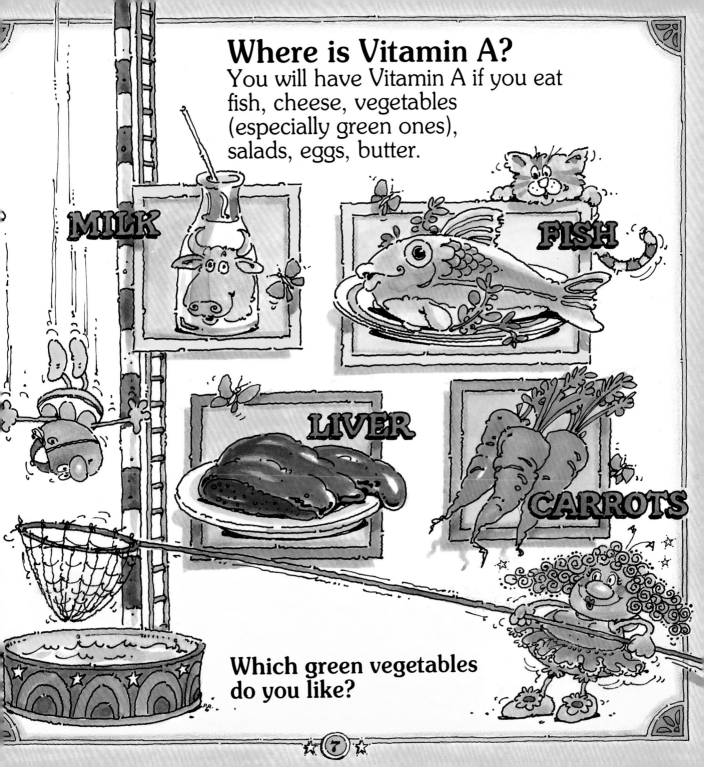

MILK

FISH

LIVER

CARROTS

Which green vegetables do you like?

We are the Vitamin B's.
There are nine of us and we are very important while you are growing.

We all work together to look after your muscles and your heart and we help you sleep. Some of us look after your skin and work with our friends to make sure that you have nice healthy hair.

Where are Vitamin B's?

The B Vitamins are found in bread, milk, liver, meat, marmite, green vegetables, fish, eggs, cereal, rice, yoghurt, beans, soya.

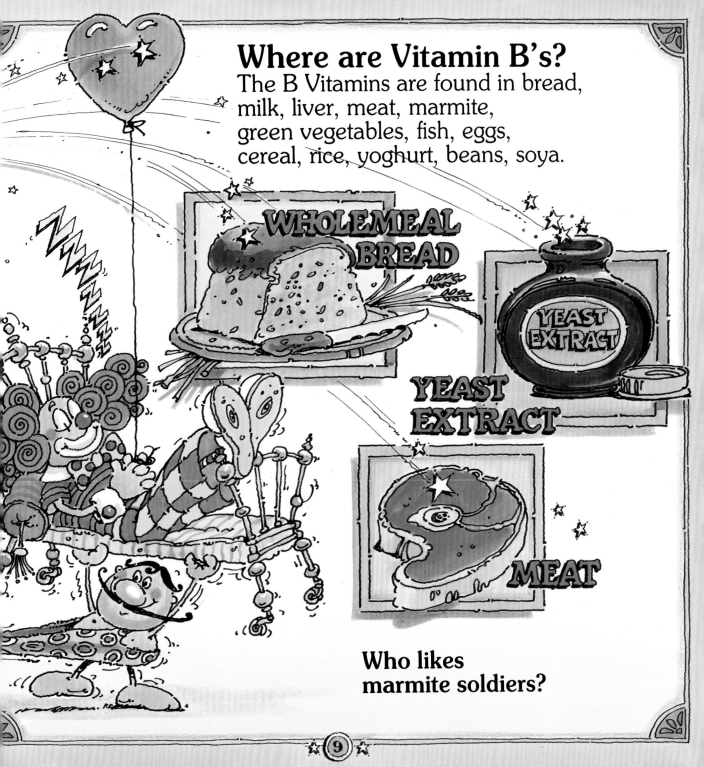

WHOLEMEAL BREAD

YEAST EXTRACT

YEAST EXTRACT

MEAT

Who likes marmite soldiers?

Chloe

I am the nurse vitamin.

I help you to get better when you are hurt, and I stop you getting too many coughs and colds. (who helps me?)

Where do we find Vitamin C?

All fresh fruit and vegetables have vitamin C in them. Milk has a little but if it gets warm in the sun the Vitamin C might disappear, so keep it in the fridge.

VITAMIN C

VITAMIN C

APPLES

TOMATOES

ORANGES

How many vegetables can you think of?

Carbohydrate is my name and that is very long so you can call me Colin. You need me to give you energy so that you can play football, skip, run races and play games with your friends without getting tired.

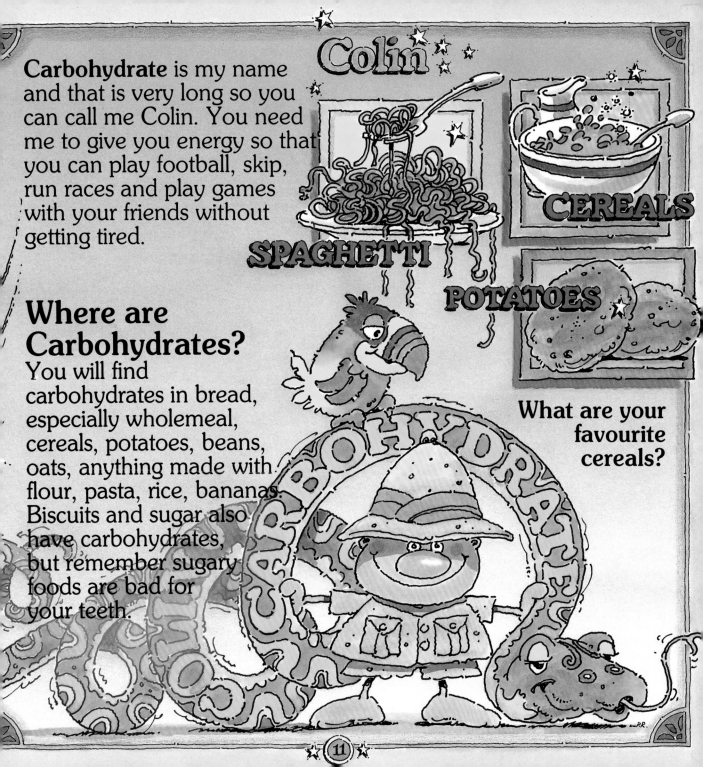

Colin

SPAGHETTI

CEREALS

POTATOES

Where are Carbohydrates?

You will find carbohydrates in bread, especially wholemeal, cereals, potatoes, beans, oats, anything made with flour, pasta, rice, bananas. Biscuits and sugar also have carbohydrates, but remember sugary foods are bad for your teeth.

What are your favourite cereals?

Cassie Calcium

I like my name Cassie Calcium and I am important to you when you are growing.

If you don't have enough of me your bones won't be strong. Your muscles won't work properly and your little teeth won't be healthy and white.

Where can you find me?

Cheese, bread, flour, yoghurt, nuts, baked beans, green vegetables, tofu.
All these have calcium but milk has most of all.

MILK

CHEESE

FRUIT YOGGI

YOGHURT

Think of all the ways you can have milk.

I am dancing Vitamin D

and I work with Cassie Calcium to make your bones and teeth grow strong.

Where is Vitamin D?

Oily fish, liver and dairy foods have vitamin D in them, but Mr Sun has most of all.

Sunlight (don't get sunburn) makes Vitamin D when it touches your skin.

SARDINES

VITAMIN D VITAMIN D

MILK

Which dairy foods do you know?

Helpful Vitamin E that's me.

I help all the other vitamins with their jobs.
Without me the others couldn't do their work properly.

Eric **Where do you find Vitamin E?**

Eggs, bread, butter, wholewheat, green vegetables, sunflower oil, cereals.

PEANUT BUTTER

EGGS

CEREALS

How do you like your eggs?

Fernando

I'm Fats Fernando.

When you are older, too much fat is not good for you. But when you are very young you need some fat to help you grow properly (but not piles of chips and crisps).

CHOCOLATE

CHOCCY C...

Which foods have Fats?

Butter, margarine, meat are the ones you know but did you know that there is fat in milk, chocolate, cakes, cheese, eggs, crisps.

HIPS & SAUSAGE

CAKES

Colin Carbohydrate and some other vitamins need me to help them to do their work.

Which are your favourite cakes?

I'm Freddie Fibre the cleaner.

I don't have any nutrients but without me your food
won't find it easy to get where it is needed.
You don't need as much of me
as grown-ups do.

ibre

Where is Fibre?

Vegetables and fruit,
especially when uncooked.
Bread especially wholemeal.
Shredded wheat and bran.
If you have potatoes in
their jackets you get more
fibre.

BAKED BEANS

BANANAS

JACKET
POTATOES

What fillings do you like in jacket potatoes?

FOOD GROUPS

All the food you eat can be put into four groups.

For every meal
Remember to have one thing from at least three of the groups.

Every day
Try to have at least one thing from all of the groups.

WHAT ARE THE FOUR GROUPS?

1 FRUIT & VEGETABLES

2 DAIRY FOODS

3 MEAT & FISH

4 BREAD & CEREALS

Think what you have eaten today. See which groups the food was from.

1 Fruit and Vegetables

Apples, oranges, pears, kiwi fruit, all salad vegetables, fresh and frozen vegetables, cabbage.
All types of fresh or frozen fruit and vegetables have vitamin C in them so try and have some every day.

3 Meat & Others

Meat, fish, chicken, turkey, eggs, sausages, bacon, ham.
If you don't want to eat meat here are some foods that you can eat instead.
Beans, lentils, baked beans, tofu, nuts, tahini.

2 Dairy Foods

Milk, cheese, yoghurt, fromage frais, quark, cottage cheese.
If you don't like drinking milk, try to eat yoghurt or cheese.
One small yoghurt or 1oz. of cheese is worth $\frac{1}{3}$ of a pint of milk for calcium.

4 Cereals

Bread, chapati's, pitta, naan, breakfast cereals, pasta, rice, potatoes, porridge.

Over the next few pages there is more about the foods in each group.

HEALTHY DRINKS

What are Healthy Drinks?

Fresh fruit juices,
cold milk, or water are nice
refreshing drinks.
If you like your drinks fizzy
you can mix fruit juices with
sparkling mineral water.

Everyone needs to drink, not just to stop you feeling thirsty but to keep your body working properly.
You can have lots of nice drinks but remember that too many fizzy and sugary drinks are bad for your teeth.

FRUIT JUICE

MILK

WATER

How many delicious drinks can you make?

Hello I'm Ivan Iron.

My job is to look after your heart and your blood. I make sure that you have nice rosy cheeks and stop you feeling tired when you want to run around and play.

What has Iron?

Bread, vegetables, beansprouts (fresh), meat, eggs and cereal.

If you don't eat meat, then eggs, green vegetables and orange juice are very important because Chloe C helps Ivan Iron with his work.

MEAT

SPINACH

CORNFLAKES

What other fruit juices do you like?

Kelly

I'm Vitamin K
You need me to be around when you cut yourself to make sure you stop bleeding.

VITAMIN **K** VITAMIN **K**

Where would you find Vitamin K?
Vitamin K is found in most leaf green vegetables. Tomatoes and meat also have some.

CAULIFLOWER

BRUSSEL SPROUTS

LETTUCE

How many green vegetables can you think of?

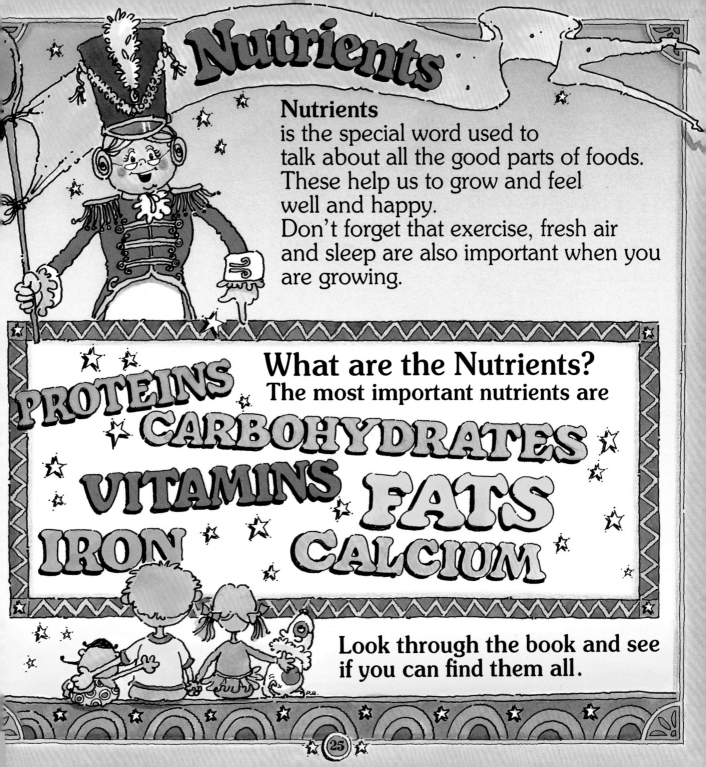

Nutrients

Nutrients
is the special word used to
talk about all the good parts of foods.
These help us to grow and feel
well and happy.
Don't forget that exercise, fresh air
and sleep are also important when you
are growing.

What are the Nutrients?
The most important nutrients are

PROTEINS

CARBOHYDRATES

VITAMINS FATS

IRON CALCIUM

Look through the book and see
if you can find them all.

Peter Protein

My name is Peter Protein and I am the builder and repairer. Everyone's body is made of millions of little cells. I help to build these and when you hurt yourself you damage cells and I have to mend them. I can also help to give you energy.

Where is Protein?
Meat, fish, chicken, milk, nuts, cheese, bread, cereal, beans

CHICKEN

FISH

MILK

**What is your favourite food with protein in it?
Do you like beans on toast?**

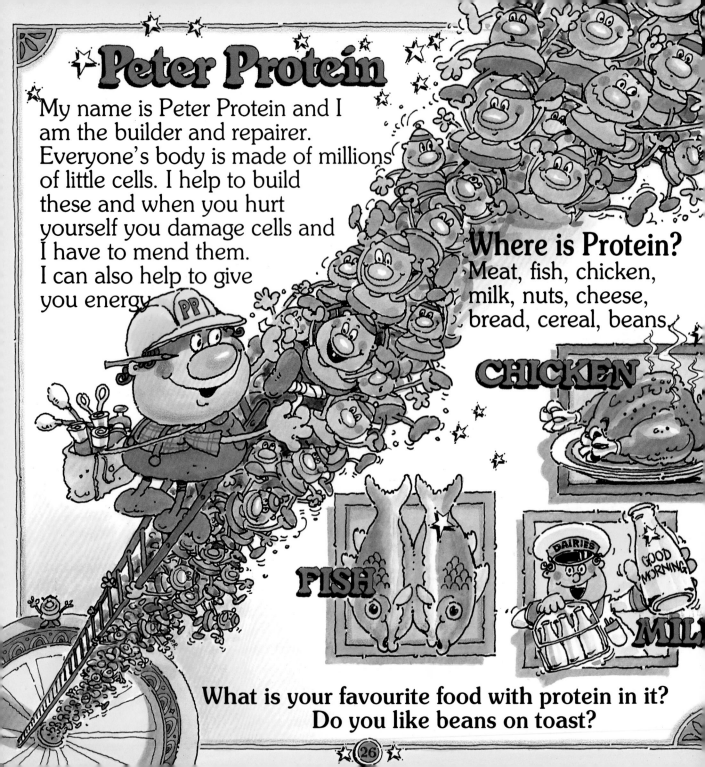

Sally Sugar

Sally Sugar is my name and I give you energy. Remember that too much of me can spoil your teeth. Think of other things with carbohydrates to give you energy.

If you eat sugary things remember to clean your teeth afterwards and never have sugary food or drinks just before you go to bed.

Which foods have Sugar?

We don't just find sugar in a bag, it is in lots of things like cakes and chocolate biscuits. Some fizzy drinks and squashes have sugar in them.

Did you know that fruits like apples and oranges have sugar in them?

TOFFEE APPLES

CHOCOLATE BISCUITS

FIZZY DRINKS

How many different fruits do you know?

Sammy Salt

Although you need me Sammy Salt to keep your body working, lot's of food already has me in it, so there is no need to go sprinkling salt from the pot all over your dinner.

What is Sammy Salt in?

A lot of food that you probably never thought about has salt in it like milk, nuts, eggs, pickles, butter, herrings, cereals, bacon, salami and of course most potato crisps have some salt.

PORK PIES

SAUSAGES

CRISPS

READY SALTED

CRISPS

Treats

All of you like treats and everyone has their own special favourites.
Try to keep sweet and fizzy things as treats so that you don't have too many. Then you will enjoy them more and you won't harm your teeth.

Your own treats

What are your special treats to eat and drink?
When is the best time to have treats?

Let's find out

Look in your alphabet and find out:

1 Which foods give you energy?

2 Which is the nurse vitamin?

3 Which foods have most nutrients?

4 Some of the nutrients work together to do their jobs. Can you find some that do?

5 If there are many foods that you don't like what can you eat instead?

6 Sandwiches are easy to eat. Think of some nice fillings that have the right nutrients in them.

WHAT SHALL WE EAT TODAY?

BREAKFAST

a very important meal.

Cornflakes with milk
Orange juice
Boiled egg with bread
and butter fingers

MIDDAY

Beans on toast
Yoghurt
Apple
A drink of water
with fruit juice

EVENING

Chicken
Jacket Potato, Green
Banana
Glass of milk

**Now you decide
what you would like.**

Remember the four food groups.

Important Things to Remember

1 Children are growing fast so they need:

PROTEIN ☆ CALCIUM ☆ IRON ☆ VITAMINS A, B, C. ☆

to help them grow.

2 Children are very active and need energy giving food.

3 Children have small stomachs and large appetites so meals should not be too bulky.

Cheese - meat - eggs - fruit and vegetables are important to give the nutrients needed.

Milk is a good way to have Calcium and Vitamins A and D.